A percentage of the sale will be donated to the Guillain Barrē Syndrome support group.

This book is available by post from:
Pendulum Gallery Press at £3.00 including postage.

ISBN 0-948912-03-0
First published 1987
by PENDULUM GALLERY PRESS
The Manse
56 Ackender Road
Alton, Hampshire.



Made and Printed in Great Britain by
MAYFLEET PRINTERS LIMITED
FLEET, HAMPSHIRE.

# WHY ME?

by

LEO GALE

ILLUSTRATIONS
by
TONI GOFFE

· PENDULUM · GALLERY ·
· PRESS ·

# WHY ME?

Before March 1985 Leo, myself and our three young children were a normal happy family living in Farnham, Surrey. Leo worked for Chubb Fire as a General Sales Manager.

During that Month Leo felt ill with all the symptoms of flu but within three days he was totally paralysed; unable to move even an eyelid. He was hospitalised and diagnosed as suffering from Guillain Barrē' Syndrome, a condition which attacks the outer covering of the nerve strands throughout the body. In severe cases like Leo's, sections of the nerves themselves can die.

He was in Frimley Park Hospital from the second of April 1985 until the middle of August when he was moved to Unsted Park a rehabilitation centre. At this stage he could not move his arms or legs and had to be lifted, fed, washed, and pushed in a wheelchair. At the end of September he moved to The Wolfson Centre another unit. By now he could stand and walk a little with great difficulty but could not use his arms or hands.

He was discharged on the fourteenth of February 1986 after spending a total of ten and a half months in hospitals and rehabilitation centres. When he came home he could feed himself with the aid of wrist splints but could not wash or dress. At the end of March 1986 he started back to work on a part-time basis, and returned full-time in July. He is still unable to use his hands properly after two years and his walking is still very painful at times.

This anthology is a tribute to Leo's determination and love of life; a thank you to his firm and all our friends for their love and support.

*Jenny Gale*

# HOSPITAL...

# WHY ME?

A question all people ask whether for
themselves or a loved one.
There is no answer.

# WHY ME?

Why me?
Did I upset the gods of love
for them to strike me from above?
I feel more loved now than ever before
it's not the gods of love for sure.

Why me?
Did I upset the gods of hate?
Did I forgive the twist of fate?
Well if that's true then mark me well
the gods of hate can go to hell.

Why me?
Did I upset the gods of life
for them to stab and twist the knife?
but I've friends, children and a beautiful wife
so it couldn't be the gods of life.

So why me?
Why not?

# THE LONELY FIGHT

Even with all the help from
doctors, nurses, friends and loved ones,
you are still very much on your own,
and the fight is yours.

# THE LONELY FIGHT

Good morning dear how are you today?
the pretty nurse would smile and say,
Yes I'm fine yes I'm OK
well what else can you really say,
that you've been crying half the night
stranded in the lonely fight.

You do look well the visitors say
better than the other day,
so you slip into the part that you have to play
and wait until they go away
there're trying to help so it wouldn't be right
to tell them it's a lonely fight.

Yesterday I said a prayer
today I'm not sure that he's there,
even worse I don't really care
if he did this, well it isn't fair
has he really got the right
to throw you into the lonely fight.

I've got to win, I've got to fight
I've got to live I have the right,
but sometimes, try as I might
I look through the tunnel but can't see the light
but I'll keep trying I'll hold on tight
and one day I'll win this lonely fight.

# HANDS

When you lose the use of a limb
it is hard to come to terms with.
I lost the use of all mine and could only
lie in bed day after day week after week
looking at my useless body, remembering
how things used to be.

# HANDS

These hands aren't my hands
these hands aren't the hands that did
these hands aren't my hands
the hands that held my kids.

These legs aren't my legs
the legs that ran and played
these legs aren't my legs
the legs that stuck and stayed.

These arms aren't my arms
the arms that held and loved
these arms aren't my arms
the arms that pushed and shoved.

These thoughts aren't my thoughts
the thoughts that made me, ME;
these thoughts aren't my thoughts
the thoughts that set me free.

But they are mine,
I know that well
but they are mine,
my private hell.

# IT'S ENOUGH

God is sometimes elusive, so then
you have to find a reason to live,
it isn't hard.

# IT'S ENOUGH

No god no fate no great design
no illusions in this world of mine
an understanding of our time
It's enough.

No miracles no magic cures
just simple folk and honest doers
places still that have their lures
It's enough.

No dream of wealth or urge for power
no memory of a plan gone sour
but the fragrance of the occasional flower
It's enough.

No hate no spite because I was right
resentment or a sleepless night
just another day in the morning light
It's enough.

No need of heaven no fear of hell
no want of a priest or a tolling bell
if I'm in the stories that my children tell
It's enough.

# SLEEP

Sleep is hard to come by in hospital,
and when you have Guillain Barre it's even harder.
In the early hours of the morning all you want to do is die.

# SLEEP

Let me sleep,
like I used to do.
Let me sleep,
and dream of you.
Let me sleep,
and forget the pain.
Let me sleep,
to escape again.
Let me sleep,
in the dreams of men.
Let me sleep,
and die, and then,
let me sleep.

# WHEEL CHAIR

I spent nine months in a wheelchair,
nothing compared to some of my friends,
but enough to understand.

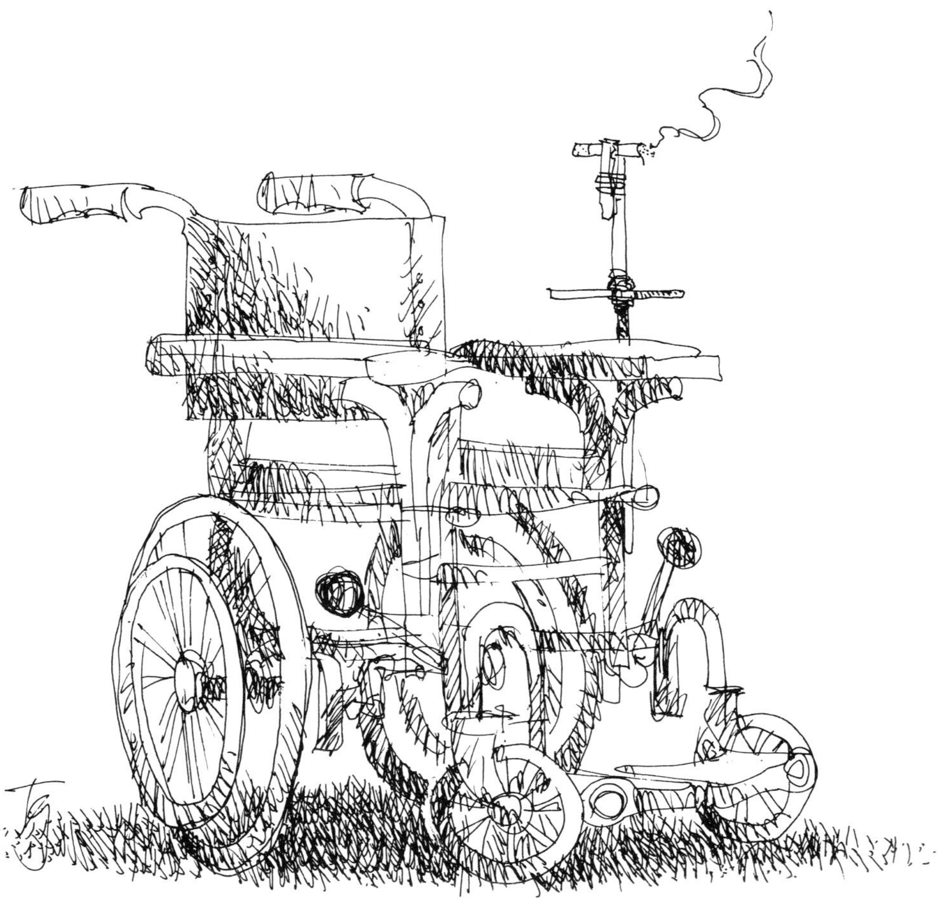

# WHEEL CHAIR

I used to walk but now I ride
with no companion by my side
and conversation seems to lack
when friends are walking at the back.

I used to walk but now I ride
it's not my fault if we collide
with peoples ankles when they stop
I'd have the pain if we could swap.

I used to walk but now I ride
my children push the chair with pride
and give their gentle love for free
I hope they feel that it's still me.

I used to walk but now I ride
and at the coast I watch the tide
and see the children on the beach
near, yet somehow out of reach.

I used to walk but now I ride
and kindly people move aside
and when they look what do they see
I see silent sympathy.

I used to walk but now I ride
emotions are so hard to hide
and even though you really try
friends and loved ones see you cry.

I used to walk but now I ride
and just in you I will confide
I'll hate this chair until the end
even though it's been a friend.

# LEAVING

When you leave hospital you are cured
and you go home – or do you?

# LEAVING

I'm leaving today but I feel sort of scared
is it leaving the Nurses the times that we shared,
Nearly five months I've laid in this bed
pumped full of pills being washed shaved and fed
lifted about from bed bath to chair
making friends with the girls who gave me the care.

I'm leaving today but I'm not well yet,
rehabilitation is what I'm out to get,
and what that's all about I'm yet to find out
but I'll know soon enough of that there's no doubt,
I've heard the odd thing like "they'll make you work",
and "they throw people out if they start to shirk".

I'm leaving today but I feel sort of sad
I'm leaving the room and the bed that I had
I'm leaving the smell and the death and the tears
the memories I'll take with me through future years.
They all came to see me and wish me goodbye,
and all I could do was sit here and cry.

I'm leaving today:

# REHABILITATION

# THE CENTRE

To enter a rehabilitation centre is a cultural shock.
Your main feeling is one of not belonging –
you soon get over it.

# THE CENTRE

My friends don't walk too well these days
they're handicapped in many ways
we're going through a funny phase,
at the centre.

Wheel chairs disappear from view
it's Peter, Harry, Fred or Sue
we'll cheer on your first step or two,
at the centre.

My friends don't talk too well these days
but that's made up in many ways
they fight for every word and phrase,
at the centre.

They cry when they come and relatives grieve
but it's a funny thing so would you believe
thet usually cry when they have to leave,
at the centre.

We smoke too much and drink a lot
let lungs corrode and livers rot
and does it matter, not a lot,
at the centre.

# GUILLAIN BARRÉ SYNDROME

If you can write humour in a north country accent
on a typewriter with a pen in your teeth,
you can do anything.

I'll tell about night of the lecture
on this sickness I have that's quite rare,
It were all about how you can spot it
and how to give folks proper care.

Doc Wilson talked all about symptoms
and how you leave nothing to chance,
about two French blokes called Guillain and Barre,
they discovered the syndrome in France.

He said that all over your body,
not on top like but right underneath,
we all have this fatty stuff over our nerves
he said it were called Myelin Sheath.

Now it seems that your own antibodies
meet up on this Myelin Sheath,
then they seem to go mad, the good ones turn bad
and they eat it away in their teeth.

They're sorry as soon as they've done it,
attacking there host as they do,
but the brain can't get signals down arms and legs
so the muscles don't know what to do.

Paralysis follows, its awful,
you can't move a finger or toe
and even though eighty percent odd get well,
recovery is painfully slow.

Then John, he's a Physiotherapist,
and knows about muscles and joints
He had tested my body all over
and had given my arms and legs points.

He said that passive movements
twice a day were a definite must
or your muscles could pack up forever
and your joints could get covered in rust.

Then it were time for my demo'
John looked at me and said, "stand",
I pushed with my legs and pressed with me arms
and it worked out just as we planned.

Then John put me over to parallel bars
and I walked up and down once or twice,
the people all clapped when I walked with no hands,
I were glad he didn't say, "do it twice".

Then the people asked all sorts of questions
they even, asked some of me
then we all finished off with a round of applause,
and then we went home for our tea.

# THE SMOKING MACHINE

Bernard was a patient I met in the centre, he had a super sense of humour and invented a smoking machine for me to fit on my wheelchair to hold my cigarettes. However the end result was less grandiose than the idea he had in his head.

# THE SMOKING MACHINE

Bernard's a thinker,
he thought me up a smoking machine
with ten cigarettes in a magazine
a lighter worked by my big toe
and an ash collector down below.

He thought it up when in O.T.*
we had to feed him cups of tea
and just to watch was such a strain
that Doctor's feared for Bernard's brain.

But then the unit was complete
with pools of sweat at Bernard's feet
and O.T's wiping him down with towelling;
a clothes peg on a piece of dowelling?
But as I said, Bernard's a thinker.

*(*O.T. is an abbreviation for Occupational Therapist.)*

# THE MAN

When you have faith in yourself most things are possible.
I discovered a strength I didn't know I had.

# THE MAN

The man said you can make it,
you're young and strong enough to take it
and in a year or two,
you'll know the man who pulled you through.

The man said keep on trying,
all over the world there are people dying
and some have not a hope,
you're the sort I know can cope.

The man said trust in me,
I'll get you well and set you free
I know he speaks the truth, you see,
the man who said it all, was me.

# WHEN ?

Sometimes things don't happen fast enough.
I could not use my arms and hands for over seven months.
Now after two years I still get very impatient at times.

# WHEN?

I'll have a shave and clean my teeth
lift things up and look underneath
write things with a pen
when.

I'll shake hands with my real true friends
applaud like hell when a concert ends
and mend the toys again
when.

Cut the grass clean the car
point up and show the kids a star
and be like other men
when.

I think I'll have to feel and touch
that's one thing that I've missed so much
will it be the same again
when.

I'll hold my wife and shed a tear
and try to pay her back this year
and try to start again
when.

Or will it be just another day
lost, without a band to play
to celebrate the day
when.

# VAL

Val was a lovely lady who I met in the centre,
she was dying of a rare muscle wasting disease.
She died in October 1986 leaving a son and daughter
and a lot of people who loved her.

# VAL

Lovely lady sitting there
taking in the evening air,
living in the freedom of her mind,
eyes closed she feels the sun
sees her daughter hears her son
wishes them the joy she left behind.

Lovely lady in the sun
the autumn of her life begun,
dreams away the springtime of her youth,
is life any dearer now,
are things and clearer now,
is she any nearer to the truth.

Lovely lady please excuse
the clumsy way these words I use,
there's just one more thing I wish to say,
thank you Val for being you,
thanks because you helped me through
I'll think about you every single day.

# WALKING AGAIN

Not a big word, but a hell of a big thing to learn again.
I was lucky.

# WALKING AGAIN

All the way from here to there
I'll be glad when I'm back in the old wheelchair,
to take this risk I must be insane
but I'm walking again.

That's it, I won't try any more
I'm back down here on the hard cold floor,
there must be something wrong with my brain
to try and walk again.

Something drives me to have a go
but when I walk it's painful and slow,
this look on my face is mental strain
but I'm walking again.

That corridor looks two miles long
I'll be back on the floor if it all goes wrong,
but I've nothing to lose and a lot to gain
by walking again.

# HOME

# JENNY

She loved me, cared for me, believed in me
and gave me the will to live.

# JENNY

How can simple words express
the way I feel for you unless,
I wrote a book with every word
as perfect as the humming bird
a thousand pages from my heart,
I know could never make a start
and even if you read it through
it could only say, I love you.

How could a painting capture you
the million things you say and do
your touch, your smile, your warmth just you
one painting that could never do
if I did a painting every day
a thousand pictures couldn't say
the way I feel for you,
I love you.

Should I write a lover's tune
a song about the stars and moon
a concerto for a thousand strings
to show the joy that each day brings
no, I'll just hold you in my arms
enjoy again your many charms
there is nothing more to do,
I love you.

# A FRIEND

They emerge from nowhere and stay.

# A FRIEND

Is a friend a woman
or is a friend a man
does a friend say "no you can't"
or "come on yes you can".

Is a friend your conscience
or the demon held within
delivering you from evil
or leading you into sin.

Is a friend a listener
to tell your troubles to
or is a friend a problem
who always turns to you.

Is a friend a prison
or a way to set you free
if your thoughts are ever with me,
then you're a friend to me.

# GROWING

My children had to grow up fast, but then we all did.
In the end you have little choice.
You have to learn to cope, and to start again.

# GROWING

The love that is sought by a child,
the pleasure in just running wild,
the longing, the yearning,
the boredom of learning,
and the growing.

The fleeting perfection of youth,
the gradual learning of truth,
the hurt and the pain,
and the trying again,
and the growing.

the arrogance in the young man,
the need to say, your wrong, I can,
the crying, the bending,
the pleasure in mending,
and the growing.

The maturing comfort of age,
the strength to turn a new page,
the joy in just living,
the peace in forgiving,
and the growing.

# THE BOY

Watching my children grow makes me remember my own childhood, when the only complication was getting home on time.

# THE BOY

The river was running fast
as the boy went running past,
then he stopped and turned around
and headed for the rushing sound.

His ships were only broken twigs
he didn't need the sails and rigs
and battles fought were always won,
losing's never any fun.

The fleet sailed out he heard a band
he held his cutlass in his hand,
"The country's lost," he heard them say,
"unless our hero wins the day."

The battle soon was fought and won
and medals stuck with chewing gum
were placed upon our hero's chest
"it's nothing sire, I did my best."

The river was running fast
and more time than he thought had passed,
now he faced a different fate,
dinner time and he was late.

# THE ART

Life is a puzzle.

# THE ART

How do we learn the art of life
to cope with all the pain and strife
to laugh, to love, to make a friend
is it at the start or at the end.

When do we learn the darker arts
the blacker side to all our hearts
to hurt; and wound; and scar;
or is that taking life too far.

Do poets, learn, the art of rhyming
do actors, learn, the art of timing
do we ever really start
to learn the art.

When we do learn to play our part,
at the end; or at the start
and how do we see it as a whole
when each of us plays the leading role.

# A NEW BEGINNING.